Dad,

More than you know, when I look back over the time we've shared, I see your *support*... I see your *care*... I see your *generosity*. It's clear how much *your love* has shaped me.

These days I'm so grateful for who we've become— for the ways we show up for each other. For everything we get to be.

More than you know, I look forward to all that's still to come. Because Dad, you mean *the world* to me.

Love,

_____

MORE

THAN

EVER...

I LOOK BACK AND LOVE ALL THE ORDINARY THINGS
AND THE SIMPLE ROUTINES.

All those times we

_____

_____

_____

have become some of my
favorite memories.

Thank you
for the
ways
you cared
for me...

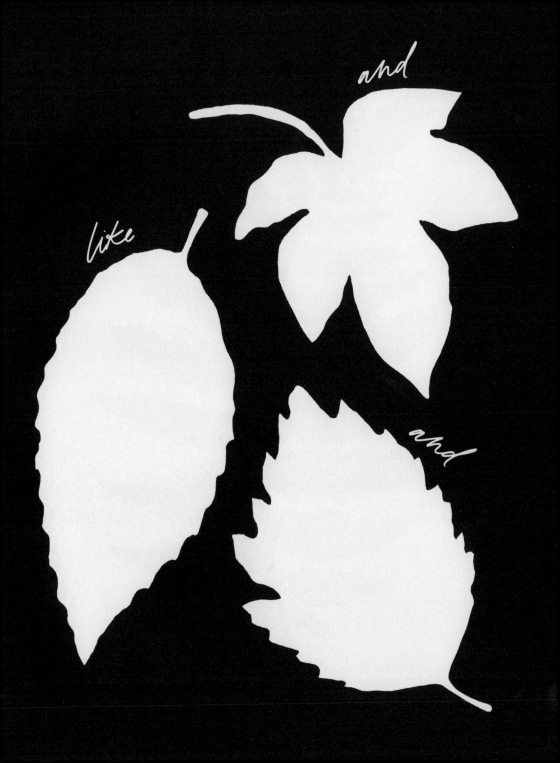

You might think

_____

_____

_____

was just a little thing.
But it always felt like *magic* to me.

Dad, from the very beginning, I *believed* you could

_____

_____

_____

AND THE TRUTH IS, I STILL DO.

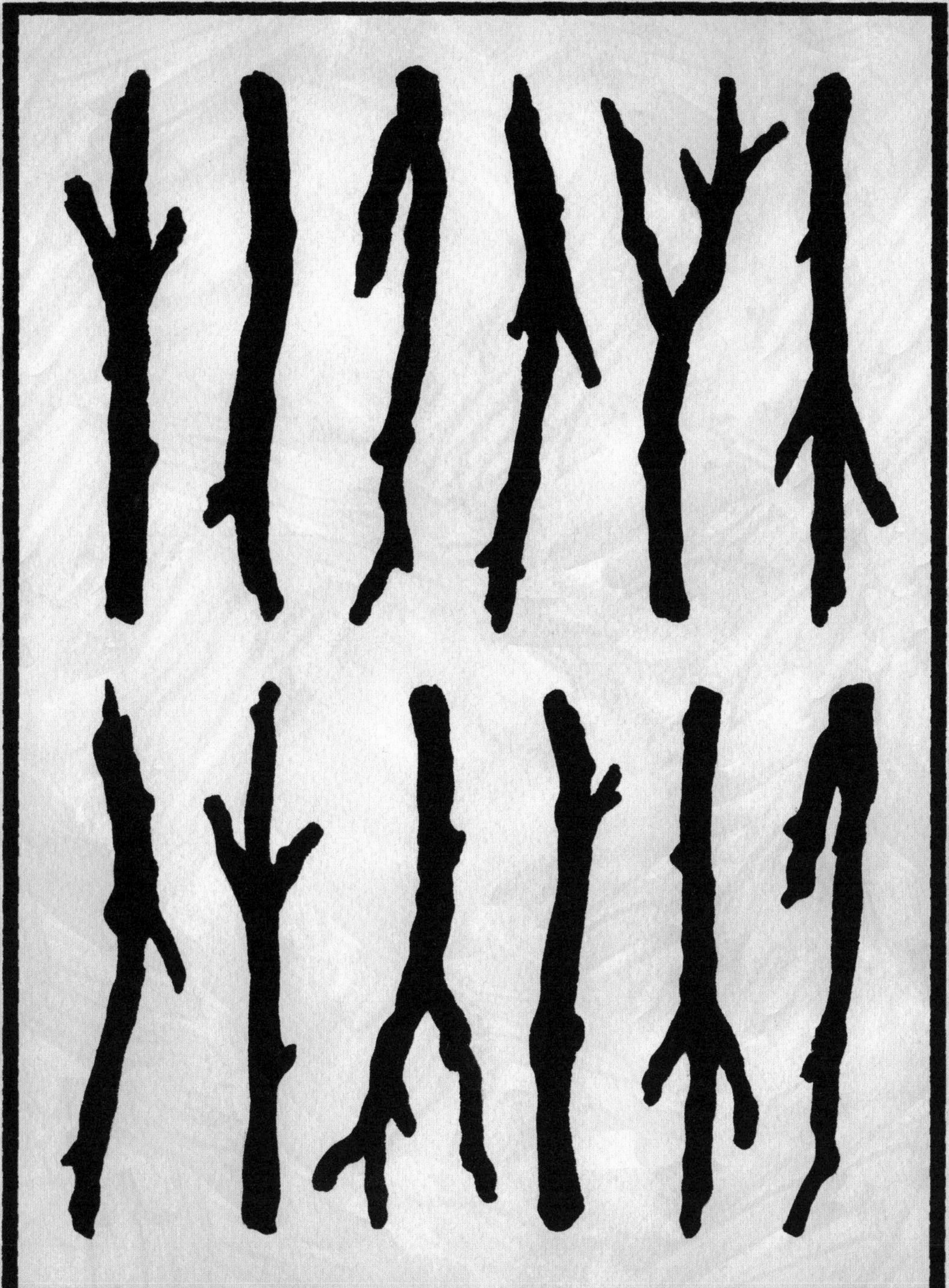

I thought all families

_____

_____

_____,

but it turns out that
was *just us*.

WHICH MAKES ME FEEL REALLY LUCKY.

I realize now that no one ever
had to teach me

_____

_____

_____

I learned
just by
watching
you.

I love the way we

▄▄▄▄▄▄▄▄▄▄▄▄▄▄▄▄

▄▄▄▄▄▄▄▄▄▄▄▄▄▄▄▄

▄▄▄▄▄▄▄▄▄▄▄▄▄▄▄▄

It's one of the most *important*

things we share.

MORE THAN YOU KNOW...

I APPRECIATE THE THINGS I'VE INHERITED FROM YOU.

Like *your* love of

_____

_____,

and *your* ability to

_____

_____.

I'm so glad you *instilled* in
me *the belief* that

_____

_____

_____

When
I think about
how similar we are,
it's usually
because...

and

I think

_____

_____

_____

is one of the gifts you offer the world,
so often, and *so generously.*

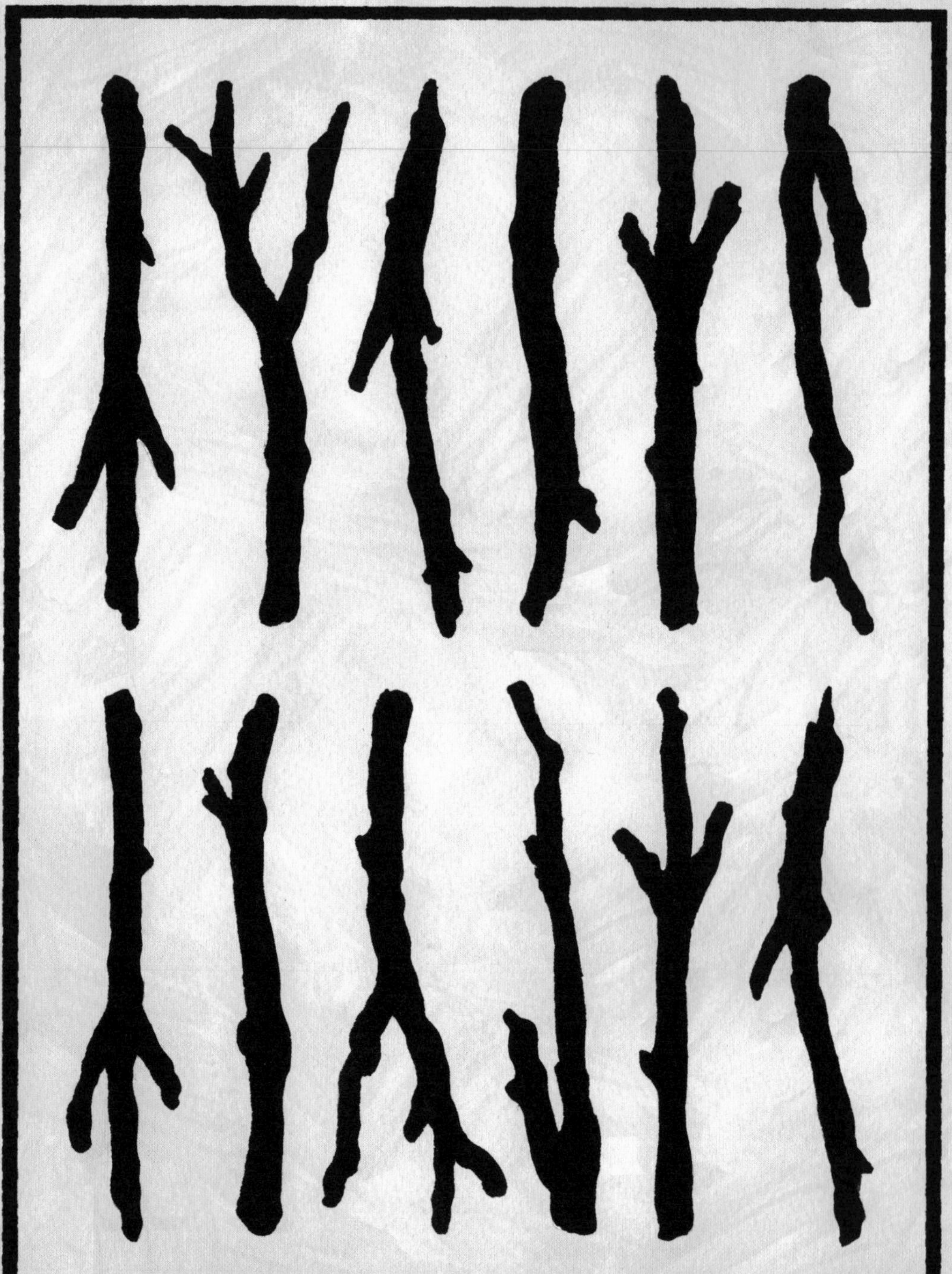

Dad, *thank you* for
giving me space to

_____

_____

_____ ,

even when you
didn't always agree.

When I look back on it,
I can see how *hard you worked* to

_____

_____

_____

I feel so
grateful to
realize
that without
you,

I don't think I *ever* would have

_____

_____

_____

MORE THAN YOU KNOW...

There are certain *days* and *memories* I wish
we could live again and again, like

_____

_____

_____

I love
the traditions
we share.

DAD, THERE ARE CERTAIN THINGS YOU USED TO SAY
THAT I CARRY WHEREVER I GO.

Like the way you always
used to *remind me*

_____

_____

_____

As time goes on,
we get better and better at

_____

_____

_____

And
that's an
incredible
thing.

WHO WE GET TO BE TOGETHER MATTERS SO DEEPLY.

In my mind, the way we

_____

_____

_____

is what *truly* makes
us family.

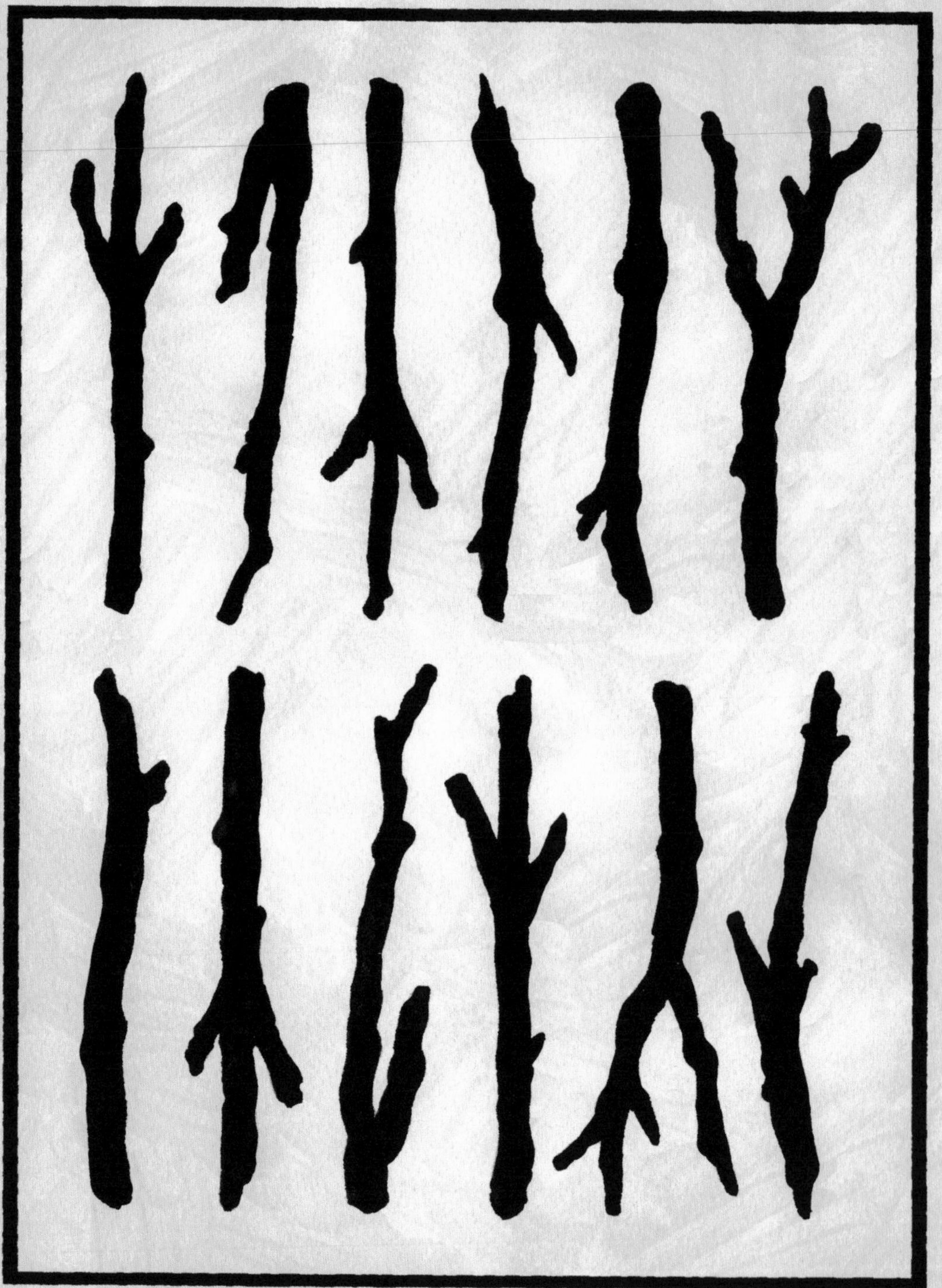

Looking back,

_____

_____

_____

was *always* one of the ways
I knew *how much* you cared.

Dad, the way you *supported* my

_____

_____

_____

has meant the world to me.

MORE THAN YOU KNOW...

You have so many qualities I look up to.

I've always *admired* the way you

_____

_____

_____

No
matter
where
I am,

I love the way that

_____

_____

_____

still makes me *think* of you.

The older I get, the more I
appreciate your *one-of-a-kind*

_____

_____

_____

I hope
we can
always make
time for...

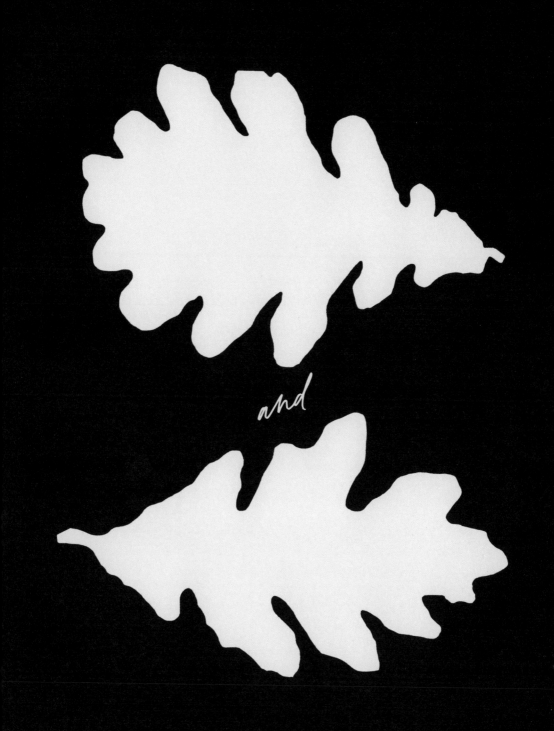

and

One of the *most important* things

you've ever taught me is that love means

_____

_____

_____

Dad, more than you know,

_____

_____

_____

COMPENDIUM.
live inspired

Written by: M.H. Clark
Designed by: Chelsea Bianchini
Edited by: Amelia Riedler

ISBN: 978-1-970147-56-8

1st printing. Printed in China with soy inks on FSC®-Mix certified paper.

Create meaningful moments with gifts that inspire.

CONNECT WITH US
live-inspired.com | sayhello@compendiuminc.com

@compendiumliveinspired
#compendiumliveinspired